How did Charles Dickens get the idea to write *A Christmas Carol*? What was life like for kids in the orphanages and workhouses of Victorian England? How did children from wealthy families spend their time?

Find out the answers to these questions and more in . . .

Magic Tree House® Research Guide

RAGS AND RICHES

A nonfiction companion to
A Ghost Tale for Christmas Time

It's Jack and Annie's very own guide to children in the time of Charles Dickens.

Including:
- Chimney sweeps
- Victorian toys
- Schools for rich and poor kids
- Pickpockets

And much more!

Here's what people are saying about the Magic Tree House® Research Guides:

Your Research Guides are a great addition to the Magic Tree House series! I have used Rain Forests *and* Space *as "read-alouds" during science units. Thank you for these!!*—Cheryl M., teacher

My eight-year-old son thinks your books are great—and I agree. I wish my high school students had read the Research Guides when they were his age. —John F., parent and teacher

And from the Magic Tree House® website:

My son loves the Research Guides about knights, pirates, and mummies. He has even asked for a notebook, which he takes with him to the museum for his research.—A parent

The Research Guides have been very helpful to us, as our daughter has an abundance of questions. Please come out with more. They help us help her find the answers to her questions!—An appreciative mom and dad

I love your books. I have a great library at home filled with your books and Research Guides. The [Knights and Castles] *Research Guide really helped me do a report on castles and knights!*—A young reader

Magic Tree House®
Research Guide

RAGS AND RICHES:
KIDS IN THE TIME
OF CHARLES DICKENS

A nonfiction companion to
A Ghost Tale for Christmas Time

by Mary Pope Osborne
and Natalie Pope Boyce

illustrated by Sal Murdocca

A STEPPING STONE BOOK™
Random House 🏠 New York

Visit us on the Web!
MagicTreeHouse.com
www.randomhouse.com/kids

Educators and librarians, for a variety of teaching tools, visit us at
www.randomhouse.com/teachers

Library of Congress Cataloging-in-Publication Data
Osborne, Mary Pope.
Rags and riches : kids in the time of Charles Dickens / by Mary Pope Osborne
and Natalie Pope Boyce ; illustrated by Sal Murdocca. — 1st ed.
    p.   cm. — (Magic tree house research guide)
"A Stepping Stone book."
ISBN 978-0-375-86010-2 (trade) — ISBN 978-0-375-96010-9 (lib. bdg.)
1. Poor children—Great Britain—History—19th century. 2. Children—Great
Britain—Economic conditions. I. Boyce, Natalie Pope. II. Osborne, Mary
Pope. Ghost tale for Christmas time. III. Title.
HV751.A6 O83 2010   362.740941'09034—dc22   2009052848

Printed in the United States of America
10 9 8 7 6 5 4 3 2 1

For Diane Landolf, with gratitude

Historical Consultant:

Professor ANDREW H. MILLER, Director of Victorian Studies, Indiana University.

Education Consultant:

HEIDI JOHNSON, Earth Science and Paleontology, Lowell Junior High School, Bisbee, Arizona.

Very special thanks to the wonderful Random House team: Gloria Cheng, Mallory Loehr, Liam Hart, and especially to our tireless editor, Diane Landolf.

RAGS AND RICHES

Contents

Dear Readers,

   After we traveled to Victorian England and met the famous author Charles Dickens in <u>A Ghost Tale for Christmas Time</u>, we wanted to find out more about him and kids in his time. So off we went to the library to check out books about Charles and his world. Then we searched our computers for everything we could find about kids in London, England, where he lived. We learned that in the 1800s, London was the largest and richest city in the world. We also learned that the city was

overcrowded and filled with poor people who suffered a lot, especially kids.

We were amazed by their lives and hope you will be, too. So get your notebooks and your pencils, and let's jump on a steam train for Charles Dickens's England.

Jack

Annie

1

Hard Times for Kids

In the 1800s, England was a very powerful country. The city of London was the largest, richest city in the world. Signs of the city's wealth were everywhere. Parks, stores, factories, and beautiful buildings filled the city. Down by the wharves, hundreds of workers built ships that sailed all over the world. Factories ran night and day, turning out things like cloth, beer, furniture, and watches. London was growing, and the number of people in the city was growing as well. New buildings seemed to go up overnight. As the city grew, many people made money and lived very well.

But there was another side of London. While the city was rich, it was also poor. Terrible slums stood only blocks away from beautiful mansions. While some people ate at fancy restaurants, others were hungry, homeless, and sick. As wealthy children visited parks or museums, gangs of poor children roamed the streets, selling anything they could find, and sometimes even stealing. Why was life so hard for these children? What caused such terrible poverty in this rich city?

The Industrial Revolution
For thousands of years, most people in England lived in the country. Children grew up on farms and in small villages. They

worked alongside their parents on their farms or in village shops. Parents treated them like little adults. Even though children worked hard, they were with their families or other people they knew.

This country life changed in the late 1700s. The *Industrial Revolution* had begun in England. Much of the old way of

Industrial is a word that refers to work done by machinery in factories. **Revolution** is a change that happens quickly.

England was the first country to have lots of factories.

15

life came to an end, and things were never the same again.

The Industrial Revolution started around 1790 and lasted until the early 1900s. The discovery of steam engines helped to start it. In the past, factories used river water to power their machines. Steam engines made it possible to build factories anywhere, not just next to rivers.

Factories and mills sprang up in towns and cities all over England. Thousands of people left the countryside hoping to find work in them.

Trains Speed Things Up

For most of the 1800s, there were no cars. People walked or used horses and boats to get around. Traveling anywhere took a lot of time. This problem was solved by steam-powered trains. They made it possible to get places quickly. A trip that used to take days could now be made in hours.

Person walking fast = 4 miles per hour

Horse-drawn carriage = 10 miles per hour

Trains = 30–40 miles per hour

By 1854, thousands of miles of train track connected cities and towns to one another. Trains became the most popular way to travel and to ship products from the factories. Trains puffed in and out of London night and day, carrying hundreds of people.

Industrial Revolution
Steam engine
New factories everywhere
People move from the country
Trains

Problems for the Poor

By 1850, half of all the people in England lived in cities such as London. Because London was not prepared for these great numbers, housing was a problem. Those who could not afford houses crowded into run-down buildings, many sharing only a few rooms. Factory jobs paid little, and often people could not find jobs at all.

Thousands of children roamed the London streets with no home of their own.

Poor kids worked in factories just like adults. The factory owners did not know or care about the kids. If a child got sick, there were always other children who needed jobs. In the early 1800s, many children began working when they were five or six years old. The workday could last twelve hours or more, six days a week. For this they received only a few pennies.

Throughout the nineteenth century, there were people who tried to help kids. In the early 1830s, there were new laws to make children's workdays shorter. By the end of the 1800s, it was against the law to hire very young children. Factory conditions had improved, and fewer children worked. In 1890, the government said that all children had to go to school until they were ten years old. The schools were free

and gave many children a chance to learn to
read and write. But life for a lot of children
was still very hard.

Lewis Hine was a famous photographer who
took this picture of American factory
children so small, they had to climb up on the
spinning machine to repair broken threads.

Workhouses

Many of the children who worked in factories came from *workhouses*. The very poor could move to a workhouse if they had no home or money. Workhouses were not meant to be nice places to live. They were built to encourage people to work.

In exchange for work, people were given food and a place to sleep. Unless they were too old or sick, everyone in the workhouse had to work. Some cooked and cleaned at the workhouse. Others worked in factories or at other jobs. Even though workhouses were meant to help people,

The Marylebone Workhouse took in homeless men, women, and orphans. It could hold about 2,000 people.

many were dirty and overcrowded. In some there was barely enough to eat, and children and women were beaten.

Factory owners often used children from the workhouses. They paid the people who ran the workhouse for each child they got from them. These children did not get paid and had to sign contracts saying that they would remain in the job for as long as they were needed. In many ways it was like being sold into slavery.

In order to give homeless children better places to live than the workhouses or the streets, a doctor named Thomas John Barnardo began setting up orphanages for them. The children lived there and were given food and clothing. They also learned skills and got an education. By the time Dr. Barnardo died in 1905, it was estimated that his homes had helped almost 60,000 children.

When Dr. Barnardo (right) started his orphanages, he wandered the streets of London at night looking for children who needed help.

Queen Victoria

England has had queens and kings for a long time. Queen Victoria was crowned in 1837 when she was just eighteen. She ruled for over sixty years. That is longer than any other English king or queen. The time during Victoria's reign is called the *Victorian era*.

Victoria ruled over the *British Empire*. An empire means that one country controls many other countries. Australia, India, Canada, and parts of Africa were some of the areas that made up the British Empire.

Queen Victoria died in 1901 when she was eighty-one years old. Because she had been their queen for so long, many people felt as if they had lost a member of their family. Today there are more statues of Queen Victoria in England than any other king or queen. There have also been many movies and books written about her life.

Queen Elizabeth II, who is queen today, is Victoria's great-great-granddaughter.

Queen Victoria; her husband, Prince Albert; and five of their nine children.

2

What Charles Dickens Saw

The famous writer Charles Dickens lived in London much of his life. Charles often took walks around the city. Sometimes he covered over twenty miles in a single day. As Charles strolled down the streets, he saw how the poor lived. He listened to the way they spoke and watched how they acted. Charles wrote books about many of these people, especially poor children who had hard lives.

Charles Dickens saw kids with no homes who slept in doorways and alleys. Even on the coldest days, these children wore tattered clothes and often went barefoot. Charles knew a lot about their troubles and felt sorry for them. Once, he had been a boy with troubles of his own.

Charles Dickens was born in 1812 in Portsmouth, England. He was the second child of John and Elizabeth Dickens. Charles's father had a good job in the navy pay office, but the family was not rich. John Dickens was a kind, cheerful man, but he was careless with his money. He was often in *debt* (DET). Being in debt means that you owe money to others. Money was always a problem for John Dickens. That made it a problem for Charles's whole family.

A Boy Who Loved Books

Charles's mother taught him to read and write. When Charles was a boy, it cost money to attend school. It was not until many years later that schools were free.

Beginning in the 1840s, people set up free schools for poor children. Some were called <u>ragged schools</u> because the students usually wore rags.

In 1817, the Dickens family moved to the city of Chatham. During this time, the Dickenses had enough money to send Charles to school. He loved books and often stayed tucked away in his bedroom reading fairy tales. While other children were playing sports, Charles lay in the grass reading. He had a rich imagination and made up stories and plays. When he grew up, Charles wrote that on windy, rainy nights, he loved to sit by the fire thinking about all the books that he'd ever read.

Charles made a toy theater. He and his sister Fanny acted out plays and sang together.

Debtors' Prison

When Charles was twelve, his world turned upside down. John Dickens had borrowed more and more money. Finally he could not pay any of his debts. In the 1800s, people who could not pay their debts were sent to debtors' prisons. Some stayed there for many years. John Dickens went to Marshalsea Debtors'

Marshalsea Debtors' Prison

The artist Frank Holl painted scenes from Newgate, a well-known prison.

Prison. The prison was a grim building with massive walls. John Dickens had to stay there until he could pay back everyone he owed.

In those days, families could live in debtors' prisons together. Because they had to sell their house and furniture, Charles's mother and younger sisters and brothers lived in prison with their father. The family was heartbroken and full of shame.

Warren's Blacking Factory

Blacking was the Victorian word for shoe polish.

Charles wrote that during this time he felt all alone with no one to help him. His father found a job for him at Warren's Blacking Factory, near the prison. Charles lived in a small rented room by himself.

This is an 1822 drawing of Hungerford Stairs, the area on the Thames where Warren's Blacking Factory was located.

The factory was in an old run-down building. As he worked, Charles could hear rats squeaking and scurrying around the rooms.

For ten hours each day, he pasted labels on jars of shoe polish. In spite of the long hours, he earned very little. On weekends, he visited his family and ran errands for his father.

After Prison

After John Dickens had been in prison a few months, a relative died and left him enough money to pay his debts. The family was free, but Elizabeth Dickens was still worried about money. She wanted Charles to continue working. John Dickens disagreed and sent Charles back to school for several more years. When he was fifteen, Charles became a lawyer's clerk. Afterward, he worked for a newspaper. It was there that he began to write for a living.

Charles never forgave his mother for trying to keep him at the factory.

Later Life

Charles became one of the most popular writers in England. Even Queen Victoria read his novels. During his lifetime, he finished twenty books and many short

Charles Dickens reads to his
daughters Mary and Kate.

Often Charles signed his works with the name Boz. It was his youngest brother's nickname.

stories, plays, and articles. Charles created amazing, colorful characters that had exciting adventures. He often wrote about children whose lives were hard. His books made people laugh and cry . . . sometimes at the same time.

When Charles was a little boy, he saw a beautiful house in the country. Its name was Gad's Hill. Charles fell in love with this house. His father told him that if he worked hard, he could buy a house just like it. Charles worked so hard that he was able to buy Gad's Hill. He lived there until he died.

Charles Dickens's books have never gone out of print. They are in bookstores today. The books include titles like *Oliver Twist, A Tale of Two Cities, David Copperfield, Great Expectations, Hard*

Times, and *A Christmas Carol*. There have also been over 180 movies and TV shows made of his works.

Charles needed a big house for his nine children!

A Christmas Carol

Charles Dickens wrote *A Christmas Carol* in 1843. It is the story of a greedy old man named Ebenezer Scrooge. One of the favorite characters in the book is a crippled boy named Tiny Tim. His father, Bob Cratchit, works for Scrooge. Scrooge pays Bob very little money. Because he is poor, Bob cannot afford a doctor for Tim. Tim will die unless he can get medical care.

During the story, Scrooge is made to realize that his life has been filled with selfishness. He changes completely. He makes sure that the Cratchit family has a good Christmas and gives them enough money to cure Tiny Tim. Scrooge is so changed that he becomes like a second father to Tim.

A Christmas Carol is one of the most popular Christmas stories in history. It has been made into plays and movies. At Christmas every year, *A Christmas Carol* can be seen on TV or on the stage. The book's message of love for others shows that after so many years, Charles Dickens still touches the lives of millions of people.

3

The London of Dickens

Charles Dickens often wrote about how London felt and looked. It was full of noise, smells, and movement. Many people thought it was the most exciting city in the world. When Charles took his walks, he had to stay alert. Thousands of horse carts and carriages clogged the streets. Sidewalks were jammed. Shoppers hurried in and out of stores while businessmen in top hats walked by beggars in rags. Street sellers set up stands and sold everything from

45

strawberries to hot baked potatoes. Shops and restaurants stayed busy. At night, the theaters were full of people who came to see the latest play.

The parks in London were popular

places to relax and stroll. People walked down paths while others rode on horseback or in carriages. Nursemaids pushed babies in strollers, and children played in the grass.

In Hyde Park, people walked and rode horses and—after 1885—bicycles.

 In a giant clock tower, a bell called Big Ben rang out every hour. It still chimes today.

A Lot of Noise!

One writer said London was always rattling, growling, and roaring.

Excitement was everywhere. Thousands of street vendors shouted out their wares. Carriage drivers called out across the streets to one another. Paperboys yelled out the news as they sold their papers. The sound of music often filled the air. Street musicians and organ-grinders played day

In 1860, there were more than a thousand organ-grinders in London.

and night, especially in poor neighborhoods. Brass bands played in the parks. Carriages and carts had iron tires and made a big racket as they clattered down the uneven pavement. If someone was sick and needed quiet, families heaped straw in front of their houses to muffle the sound. It was said that the noise was enough to drive you crazy!

The Big Stink

If the noise was bad, the smells were worse. People often threw their garbage in the streets. Open sewers flowed beside the sidewalks. In the first part of the nineteenth century, farmers drove cattle to market down the middle of the streets, and horse and cow manure was everywhere. Sheep pens in the city added to the smell.

One horse can produce eight to nine tons of waste per year!

Often people could not wash because they had no running water or bathrooms. Families often shared a single toilet with other families in their building. There is one report that 120 people had to share the same toilet.

Epidemics are illnesses that spread quickly to lots of people.

In the first half of the Victorian era, clean water was hard to get. For many, water came from drains and outdoor pumps. It was full of germs and made people sick. *Epidemics* of cholera (KAH-luh-ruh) and typhoid (TY-foyd) took many lives. In 1854, a cholera epidemic killed over 30,000 people.

In 1859, the city took action. Engineers began work on water and sewage pipes

that ran miles underground. The new sewage system helped to make both the water and the streets cleaner.

The river Thames (TEMZ), which runs through London, was badly polluted. Until the sewage system was built, the river was full of garbage and runoff from sewers and factories. At times, dead animals and dead people floated on the surface. The Thames smelled really, *really* bad.

Engineers built eighty-two miles of sewer tunnels under London.

The summer of 1858 was very hot, and the smell from the Thames was at its worst. People called this summer the Big Stink. Lawmakers fled Parliament because the smell from the nearby river was so foul. They tried hanging curtains drenched in bleaching powder in the windows and doorways, but that did not stop the smell.

Nasty Soot and Fog

Charles Dickens wrote that people always went around London blinking, wheezing, and choking. People burned coal to run factories and to heat their houses. Clouds of coal smoke billowed from chimneys, covering everything in a layer of black soot.

The bad air caused a blanket of brown or yellow smog to hover over the city. Sometimes people didn't see the sun for weeks. Even during the day, they carried

In 1878, the fog lasted from November through March.

lanterns to help them find their way down the streets. Everyone had red eyes and burning throats. Many died of lung diseases caused by breathing polluted air.

There were other dangers in the fog. In December of 1873, the smog was very thick.

Some people even drowned when they lost their way in the dark and fell into the Thames.

Rookeries

There were many nice neighborhoods in London. But there were some very bad ones as well. These were slums known as the *rookeries*. Rookeries are places where birds have their chicks. Slums got this nickname because they were crowded and noisy, just like rookeries.

In the rookeries, people lived packed together in grim, dark buildings. Bugs and rats infested the rooms. Charles Dickens wrote that many houses had broken windows covered with rags and paper. He said that dirt was everywhere and that people of all ages sat on steps smoking, fighting, or yelling at each other.

Crime

Pickpockets are thieves who steal money out of people's pockets.

One of Charles Dickens's most famous books is *Oliver Twist*. Oliver is a poor orphan boy who lives in a workhouse in London. He falls into the hands of *pickpockets*, thieves, and murderers. They try to force Oliver into a life of crime, but he is rescued and taken care of by kind people. Even though Oliver is a character in a book, there were thousands of kids just like him. Because they needed money, many stole for a living. In those days, kids of all ages were arrested and punished just like grown-ups. Until late in the century, children as young as five or six could be sent to adult prisons when they committed crimes.

One journalist wrote that in 1856, London police arrested over 73,240 people.

People had to be careful of pickpockets, who lurked in railroad stations and around open markets. Because the streetlights were weak, many streets were unsafe at night.

In the late 1800s, the police department added extra policemen. They started using fingerprinting and photography to help solve crimes. London slowly became a safer city, and the crime rate dropped.

London policemen like this one are called bobbies after Sir Robert Peel, who helped create the police force in 1829.

Costermongers

Costermongers were people who sold things from carts, stalls, and wheelbarrows. Their name came from *coster*, an old word for *apple*, and *monger*, which meant *seller*. Costermongers shouted out different things to sell their wares. Can you guess what these costermongers are selling?

1. Lily white vinegar! Lily white vinegar!
2. Pretty pins, pretty women!
3. Hot wardens, hot wardens!
4. Get your saloop here, get it here!
5. Yarmouth bloaters! Get your Yarmouth bloaters!
6. Hot chestnuts, a penny a score!

7. Pippins! Pippins!

8. Whelks! Beautiful whelks!

4

Jobs for Poor Kids

In the Victorian era, thousands of poor children worked in factories. Factory owners hired them because they worked cheaply. Children could also fit into small places adults could not.

Work in the factories could be dangerous. Most children had to stand when they worked. If they fell asleep or made a mistake, they would be beaten. Machines in the factory were so loud, they caused deafness.

63

In textile mills, the air was thick with cloth fibers and dust. Lung diseases were common and often deadly.

Girls in match factories breathed in a dangerous substance called *phosphorus* (FAHS-fur-us). Phosphorus is a chemical that lights up in the dark. Match girls had so much phosphorus on their clothes and skin that they glowed at night. But the most terrible thing about phosphorus was its fumes. They caused a disease called phossy jaw that rotted many of the girls' jaws.

Until there were laws that made factories safer, accidents were common. Sometimes children were crushed by heavy loads or by falling into the grinding teeth of the machines. Because of their size, kids in cloth factories had to

climb under the machines to fix them. Many
lost fingers and even arms.

In 1888, these people, along with 1,400 others,
mostly women and girls, took to the street to
protest conditions in match factories.

One factory girl was interviewed about her job. She said that she began work at five in the morning and did not leave until nine at night . . . that is sixteen hours! During this time, she was not allowed to talk, sit, or even look out the windows.

Not all children worked in factories. Thousands worked on the streets, doing any kind of job they could find. Boys called crossing boys cleaned up the mud and horse

A crossing boy offers to help this lady cross the street without getting dirty.

dung with twig brooms. When business was slow, they did acrobatics and ran errands. Some kids turned to stealing, while others sold flowers, muffins, strawberries, or baked potatoes.

Turn the page to find out about other jobs for Victorian kids.

Trappers and Drawers

Coal miners used carts that ran on rails to get coal out of the mines. Sometimes the tunnels were only two feet high. Mine owners hired children as young as four to crawl through them. Mines were dangerous places. Workers often died in explosions and cave-ins, or by falling down mine shafts. Miners got lung diseases from breathing coal dust. Many of these kids died before they reached twenty-five.

Some children worked as *trappers*. Trappers sat at the doors of the mine,

holding a rope tied to the door. They had to open the doors so coal carts could get through and to let in fresh air. Sitting alone in the dark was tiring. If the trappers fell asleep, a coal cart could crush their legs.

Kids who worked as *drawers* had the worst job of all. Drawers had chains tied to their waists that were attached to coal carts. They crawled on all fours through the narrow tunnels, pulling the heavy coal carts behind them. Their clothes were always wet, and their bodies were black with coal dust and often covered with sores.

Mudlarks

When the river Thames was at low tide, people searched in the mud for things to sell. Most were old women, girls, and boys. They looked for bits of rope, metal, wood, coal, or iron. These people were nicknamed *mudlarks*.

Sewers emptied into the Thames, filling it with human waste and garbage. Even in the winter, the ragged mudlarks went barefoot into the icy mud and water. Glass, nails, and other sharp things cut their feet. The kids suffered terrible infections and diseases. Some got stuck in the mud and drowned as the tide came back in.

For fun, men stood on the bridges and threw coins into the water for the mudlarks to dive after. "Dip my head in the mud for a sixpence, sir!" the kids would shout.

Today a group of men called the Society of Thames Mudlarks still looks for things in the mud. But these mudlarks work for museums. They look for old bits of London's history, such as cannons, coins, and household items. They have even found some old toys.

Climbing Boys

To keep warm, people burned coal in their fireplaces. Chimney sweeps cleaned coal dust that built up in the chimneys. They brought helpers called *climbing boys* with them. These boys were often only five or six years old. Since they were small, they could squeeze through narrow parts of the chimney.

Climbing boys climbed to the top of the chimney and swept the coal dust out on their way back down. They got cuts and bruises from the jagged bricks. To toughen up their skin, salt water was rubbed into it.

If the boys got scared and stopped climbing, the chimney sweeps jabbed their feet with pins or lit fires to keep them moving. At times climbing boys got burned or stuck in the chimneys and suffocated. It was common for the boys to get skin cancer or lung diseases from the coal dust. At the end of the day, the boys carried the coal dust away in big sacks. After dumping out their sacks, they curled up in them to sleep.

In 1864, a law finally passed that fined anyone who hired a chimney sweep under the age of twenty-one. The days of the climbing boys were at an end.

Dressmakers

Rich women hired dressmakers to make their clothes. April through July was called the Season in London, when there were lots of parties and dances. Dressmakers stayed very busy during this time.

In the 1800s, dresses had yards of lace, braid, and ribbons on them. Making them

took hours of hard work. A dress could weigh as much as thirty-seven pounds. For a while, women wore very wide skirts. They were so wide, it was hard to get through the door. A gust of wind could topple the ladies right over!

Dressmakers began working when they were fourteen. For two years, they earned no money. Instead, they had sewing lessons, food, and a place to live. Work began at dawn during the Season. Dressmakers might work twenty hours a day with few breaks. At night, the girls worked by candlelight.

Their fingers grew numb, and their eyes strained to see the stitches. The girls went to bed at two or three in the morning and dragged themselves out at dawn. The Season was on and the ladies were waiting!

Maids

Many people had maids to do the house-work. Most were women or girls who began working as young as eight years old. In many ways, these girls were luckier than other working children. They lived in the houses where they worked and were given their meals and clothes. Many grew old with the families they served.

The head housekeeper trained the girls. They followed very strict rules. Maids could not laugh or talk loudly. They had to lower their eyes, curtsy, and stand aside when-ever any member of the family passed by.

The day started at five-thirty in the morning. There were no washing machines, dishwashers, or vacuum cleaners. Maids scrubbed, mopped, and polished. They hauled coal for the fireplaces, cooked, washed, cleaned the stove, and carried buckets of hot water up to the bathrooms. At ten-thirty at night, their day was over and they went to bed.

Sometimes the girls had time off on Sunday afternoon. Then they could take walks and visit with friends or family.

5

Rich Kids

Even though London had a large number of poor kids, there were many children who had much better lives. Their parents might not have been rich, but they could afford to take care of their children. These children got an education, had toys and books, and lived in comfortable houses with their families.

When Charles Dickens took his walks, he often went down tree-lined streets with tall brick mansions on either side. Many were on private streets with gates at both ends. These were the houses of very rich

 The first house Charles owned is in London. It is a museum today.

people, such as bankers, factory owners, and businessmen. Inside the houses, the rooms shone with highly polished furniture, potted plants, richly colored rugs, and patterned wallpaper. Charles could see maids sweeping the steps or fancy carriages waiting outside the front doors. Sometimes he spotted children playing games in the gardens.

Life in the Nursery

When they were little, rich children lived in a section of the house called the *nursery*. Nurseries were usually up on the top floor. There was a night nursery and a day nursery. Children played and ate in the day nursery. They slept in a bedroom next door, which was the night nursery. Their rooms were usually cozy with carpets, toys, books, and tables and chairs made just for children.

Kids had toys like rocking horses with real horsehair, dolls, tea sets, train sets, and toy soldiers.

 Most families had six or more children.

A nanny lived in the nursery and took care of the children. Many rich kids saw their parents only for short times during

the day. Most actually knew their nannies
better than their mothers. Their nannies
bathed, dressed, and fed them. They took
them for walks, taught them manners, and
looked after their needs.

Nannies often began as young housemaids.

A proper nanny would say <u>Master</u> Jack and <u>Miss</u> Annie rather than just plain Jack and Annie.

Even though the nanny was the boss, she called the children Miss or Master along with their names as a sign of respect.

Education for Rich Children

When rich children were five years old, they studied at home with a *governess*. A governess was a woman who lived with the family. Her job was to teach reading, writing, arithmetic, and sometimes music and French. When boys were seven or eight, they left for *boarding school* and came home only for holidays. The girls continued studying at home with their governesses.

When they got to school, boys learned math, geography, Latin, and Greek. The schools were very strict. If the students disobeyed, their teachers beat them with

84

Charles Dickens's oldest son went to a famous boarding school called Eton.

a paddle. No matter how cold it was, the boys had to take cold showers and eat plain food. They were also required to play sports. Their teachers were training them to become the future leaders of England. When the boys reached sixteen, they entered a university.

At home, girls took lessons in English, French, and history. Many learned sewing, dancing, and music as well. Girls had very little freedom and were not allowed to go anywhere alone. Whenever they went for walks in the park, traveled, or shopped, their governess went with them.

At eighteen, girls finished their education. The next step was for them to marry. To meet men who might become their husbands, they went to lots of parties and dances.

Wealthy parents thought music was a
necessary part of a girl's education.

87

Rich girls almost never had careers. They were expected to grow up, marry, and have children.

Unfair! Girls couldn't go to universities until the end of the 1800s!

Sickness and Death

Rich kids were not protected from everything. In the first half of the 1800s, people knew little about health. There were no vaccinations for most diseases. Although they were better off than poor children, even rich children got sick a lot. Many did not make it to their first birthday, and a third of all deaths in London were of children under five. Almost all children had one or more serious illnesses. Kids often lost close members of their family. After a relative died, the family wore black clothes for a year or even longer.

Two of Charles Dickens's brothers and sisters died young.

Children sometimes wore <u>mourning bracelets</u> made from the hair of a dead sister or brother.

Charles Dickens knew that thousands of poor children died because their parents could not afford doctors. In 1852, the Hospital for Sick Children opened in London. Charles raised money for it and asked people to help support its work. They did, and the hospital still exists today.

By the end of the century, many discoveries had been made that helped sick people. Scientists discovered that germs caused illnesses. Doctors began to sterilize their instruments and wash their hands when they saw patients. In 1879, there was a vaccine for cholera, and later for typhoid and other diseases.

At the Seaside

When steam trains came along, people could easily get to the ocean. Summer holidays on the coasts became popular. Little fishing villages turned into vacation spots. Hotels and guesthouses sprang up, and soon piers and boardwalks lined the beaches. The rich and the not-so-rich boarded trains and headed for the water. Rich families rented houses or stayed in elegant hotels. Others rented rooms in boardinghouses.

People of all ages walked on the beach and paddled in the water. Bathing suits in the Victorian era were different from ours. Girls had to wear hats, and both girls and boys often wore woolen bathing suits that came down to their knees!

Not many people could swim. They just played around in the water.

The Victorians were very modest. Many rented small enclosed huts on wheels, called bathing machines, where they changed into their bathing suits. They did not like anyone

to see them with so few clothes on, so horses pulled the huts out into the ocean. Then the bathers could get out and paddle around.

A small flag on the bathing machine showed when someone was ready to go back to shore.

Victorian children played on the beach like kids do today. They built sand castles and collected shells. They also took donkey rides, watched puppet shows, and attended concerts on the piers. The fresh sea air was a wonderful change from the fogs of London.

Today children in England still ride donkeys at the beach.

At the end of the nineteenth century, factory workers were able to take seaside vacations. Some of the small beach towns, like Blackpool, grew into busy cities. Zoos, theaters, opera houses, and dance halls were built to entertain the huge crowds that began to arrive.

Turn the page to find out about books for Victorian children.

Books and Beatrix Potter

During the Victorian era, people realized that children were not small adults. They also realized that children needed books written just for them. Before this time, there were few children's books. Children who could read usually had the Bible or stories about how to behave. As more children learned to read, authors began to write all kinds of stories for kids.

Victorian children enjoyed fairy tales and adventure stories such as *Treasure Island* and *Alice's Adventures in Wonderland*. They read books about animals such as the horse story *Black Beauty*. Some of the most beloved animal stories were written and illustrated by Beatrix Potter.

Beatrix came from a very rich family and grew up in a big house. As a girl, Beatrix spent many hours alone drawing her pets. Among these were frogs, ferrets, a bat, and two rabbits named Benjamin and Peter. Beatrix became an expert at drawing both animals and plants. She began to write stories with her own pictures in them. Her very first book was *The Tale of Peter Rabbit*. Beatrix's stories are still popular today!

6

How Things Changed

Charles Dickens died in 1870. Thousands filed by his grave, covering it with flowers. Among these were simple bouquets from the poor, carefully tied together with strips of cloth. They had lost someone who cared about their lives. He had written about the terrible conditions in workhouses and their need for schools and medical care. He had also written about the need for better housing and a cleaner city. Thanks to Charles's work and the work of many others, life for the poor began to improve.

Thirty-one years later, Queen Victoria died at the age of eighty-one.

During Victoria's lifetime, there were exciting new discoveries in science and medicine. Victoria lived to see the use of cameras, running water in houses, flush toilets, telephones, typewriters, electric lights, bicycles, and cars. But the Victorian era was over. England was moving ahead into the twentieth century.

For many children, life in England was better than at the beginning of the nineteenth century. Because of laws that helped child workers, in 1881 only half as many kids worked in factories as in 1841. By the end of the century, children who could not pay for an education were now able to go to school.

In the late 1800s, cars began to appear on the streets. At first there were so few of them, drivers needed someone to run in front of the car waving a red warning flag.

Slowly cars replaced horse-drawn carriages. As the horses disappeared, streets

 The first traffic ticket was for driving
8 miles per hour in a 2-mile-per-hour zone.

got cleaner. Gaslights brightened up houses and streets. The world was changing, and London was changing with it.

Even today, children all over the world still have hard times. Every day, thousands die from disease, war, and hunger. Experts say that in 2007, over nine million children under the age of five died from illnesses that could have been prevented. Children in poor countries often never go to school and have to work when they are very young. Like poor Victorian children, they, too, search through the garbage for food and sleep on the streets at night.

The fight to help every child is not over. There are groups of people who are trying to help. They send doctors, nurses, teachers, and food to those who are suffering. They build houses and help teach survival skills. Like Charles Dickens, they believe that all children need a chance to grow up

safely and make their way in a better world.

Doing More Research

There's a lot more you can learn about Charles Dickens and children in his time. The fun of research is seeing how many different sources you can explore.

Books

Most libraries and bookstores have lots of books about Dickens and Victorian children.

Here are some things to remember when you're using books for research:

1. You don't have to read the whole book. Check the table of contents and the index to find the topics you're interested in.

2. Write down the name of the book. When you take notes, make sure you write

down the name of the book in your notebook so you can find it again.

3. Never copy exactly from a book.
When you learn something new from a
book, put it in your own words.

4. Make sure the book is nonfiction.
Some books tell make-believe stories about
Victorian children. Make-believe stories are
called *fiction*. They're fun to read, but not
good for research.

Research books have facts and tell true
stories. They are called *nonfiction*. A librar-
ian or teacher can help you make sure the
books you use for research are nonfiction.

Here are some books about Dickens, Queen Victoria, and kids in their time, plus some of Dickens's fiction:

- *Charles Dickens*, Extraordinary Lives series, by Peter Hicks

- *A Christmas Carol* (Usborne Young Reading) by Charles Dickens, adapted by Lesley Sims

- *The Industrial Revolution* by Mary Collins

- *Kids During the Industrial Revolution* by Lisa A. Wroble

- *Oliver Twist* (Stepping Stones Classic) by Charles Dickens, adapted by Les Martin

- *Queen Victoria*, First Book series, by Robert Green

Museums

Many museums have exhibits on Victorian children and children working during the Industrial Revolution. These places can help you learn more about life in Charles Dickens's time.

When you go to a museum:

1. Be sure to take your notebook!
Write down anything that catches your interest. Draw pictures, too!

2. Ask questions.
There are almost always people at a museum who can help you find what you're looking for.

3. Check the museum calendar.
Many museums have special events and activities just for kids!

Here are some museums with exhibits about Victorian life and working children:

- Allen County Museum, Lima, Ohio

- Boott Cotton Mills Museum at Lowell National Historical Park, Lowell, Massachusetts

- Children's Museum of Houston

- Children's Museum of Indianapolis

- Home Textile Tool Museum, Orwell, Pennsylvania

- Mark Twain House and Museum, Hartford, Connecticut

- Museum of the City of New York

- Shelburne Museum, Shelburne, Vermont

- Slater Mill, Pawtucket, Rhode Island

- Windham Textile Mill and History Museum, Willimantic, Connecticut

Movies

There are some great movies based on Charles Dickens's stories!

See if you can find these and other Dickens titles:

- *A Christmas Carol*
  from Turner Home Entertainment

- *David Copperfield*
  from BBC

- *Oliver!*
  from Sony Pictures Home Entertainment

The Internet

Many websites have lots of facts about kids in the time of Charles Dickens. Some also have games and activities that can help make learning about Victorian children even more fun.

Ask your teacher or your parents to help you find more websites like these:

- www.bbc.co.uk/schools/primaryhistory/ victorian_britain

- www.nettlesworth.durham.sch.uk/time/ victorian/vschool.html

- www.schoolhistory.co.uk/primarylinks/ victorian

- www.vam.ac.uk/moc/childrens_lives/ health_&_work/index.html

- www.vam.ac.uk/moc/childrens_lives/
parlour_games/index.html

Good luck!

Index

Don't miss Magic Tree House® #45
(A Merlin Mission)

A Crazy Day with Cobras

Jack and Annie must face venomous king cobras
in exotic India to help save a friend!

Coming January 2011!

If you're looking forward to
A Crazy Day with Cobras,
you'll love finding out the facts
behind the fiction in

Magic Tree House® Research Guide

SNAKES AND OTHER REPTILES

A nonfiction companion to
A Crazy Day with Cobras

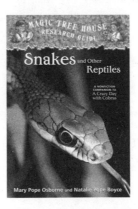

It's Jack and Annie's very own guide
to the fascinating world of reptiles!

Look for it January 2011!

Guess what?
Jack and Annie have a musical CD!

For more information about
MAGIC TREE HOUSE: THE MUSICAL
(including how to order the CD!),
visit mthmusical.com.

Magic Tree House® Books

Magic Tree House® Research Guides

More Magic Tree House®

MARY POPE OSBORNE and NATALIE POPE BOYCE are sisters who grew up on army posts all over the world. Today, Mary lives in Connecticut. Natalie makes her home nearby in the Berkshire Hills of Massachusetts. Mary is the author of over fifty books for children. She and Natalie are currently working together on more Magic Tree House® Research Guides.

Here's what Natalie and Mary have to say about working on *Rags and Riches:* "We first saw the movie *A Christmas Carol* when we were children. The picture it paints of what life in England was like when Charles Dickens was alive has always stayed with us. As we researched this book, we learned that many children during the Industrial Revolution had difficult lives. We also learned that even if children came from rich families, they often died young from diseases. Many countries, including the United States, had child factory workers in the nineteenth century. It was a new time with new problems, and people were often mistaken in the way they treated children. Today, many countries have rules that prevent young children from working. But there are still places all over the world where children work under terrible conditions."

SAL MURDOCCA is best known for his amazing work on the Magic Tree House® series. He has written and/or illustrated over two hundred children's books, including *Dancing Granny* by Elizabeth Winthrop, *Double Trouble in Walla Walla* by Andrew Clements, and *Big Numbers* by Edward Packard. He has taught writing and illustration at the Parsons School of Design in New York. He is the librettist for a children's opera and has recently completed his second short film. Sal Murdocca is an avid runner, hiker, and bicyclist. He has often bicycle-toured in Europe and has had many one-man shows of his paintings from these trips. He lives and works with his wife, Nancy, in New City, New York.